The
Report Card

The
Report Card

No Child Left Behind

TERRY OSTROSKI

To order additional copies of this book, contact:
Xlibris Corporation
1-888-795-4274
www.Xlibris.com
Orders@Xlibris.com
41584

Table of Contents

DEDICATION

I'd like to dedicate this writing to Helen Yinshanis and Carole Jean Frawley. Helen was my good friend and colleague who gave me support and encouragement in my family life and my school world. Carole Jean, my daughter and a Music teacher at Fairfield Woods Middle School in Connecticut, was instrumental in assisting me in putting this book together.

Other people who helped me after my retirement were the doctors that guided me through health problems. This enabled me to continue to develop my ideas that went into writing this book: Dr. Anthony Berger in New Britain, doctors from UCONN Medical Center Dr. Bea Tendler and Dr. Michael Dahn.

I would also like to thank my co-workers that taught with me and helped develop our first cluster programs at Washington Junior High School in New Britain, Connecticut: English teacher Robert Francini, Math teacher Walcot (Bud) Phelps, and Science teacher Peter Kummer.

Lastly, but most importantly, my family: sons Stephen Ostroski, Michael Ostroski and my husband Gene Orland Ostroski who supported me in all my endeavors.

Prologue

What is lacking in our Educational system today? A great majority of our students lag behind previous students and students around the world in scholastic excellence. The United States has pushed forward in many areas of education, but a great percentage of students do not measure up to grade standards.

The reasons are too many to count or list.

How DO we improve our schools so that these students are not left behind and that they will be able to achieve grade standards?

We certainly have not done so in recent years, especially in the Public schools. There has been plenty of money spent on new innovative programs to address these problems. Have these efforts worked or achieved the desired goals? Absolutely NOT!

What then should we do?

After spending the greater part of my life in school as a student and a teacher, I've come to the conclusion that there is only one way to go. Schools must catch up with the fast moving currents of technology and processing. Standards and policies have changed rapidly but not so in the schools. Students and teachers adhere mostly to the iron clad structure of early classes and early dismissal to rush home or away from school to do what? Most parents are not home at that time in the middle of the afternoon. Usually both parents are working away from home and students are left to their own devices. A few students attend worthwhile activities properly supervised, but most do not. Their activities consist of worthless TV talk shows; raiding the local stores; unsupervised parties at home or gathering in vacant buildings or in groups hanging out on street corners.

In view of the recent developments of the September 11 attack on our country, we must make more of an effort to instruct and toughen up our young people so that they will be prepared to face the future both physically and mentally to cope with our country's enemies.

We cannot fight terrorism or even face it if our young citizens are not prepared. The future of this country is in the hands of our young people to preserve Democracy and our freedoms in order to save America. Well-structured schools could help do that job.

My new book, entitled, "The Report Card ", will try to trace Public School environment and curriculum as it developed from about the 1930's to 2000, through the eyes and experiences of a small girl growing up in a rural community tucked into the Alleghany mountains in Pennsylvania.

At that time, students followed a strict basic curriculum that was not only instructional but led students to think and to solve problems. Schools also prepared students to face and cope with problems during World War II both pre and post. Results were evident. Through the efforts and patriotism of these young people, the allies won the war and then proceeded to build a booming economy that made the United States the leading country in the world.

Now it is time to step into the future and revise our school system in order to keep up with the new technology and the troubled world of today.

These students must have a chance in Public Schools to conquer basic studies. This will enable them to study subjects that are paramount in shaping their future careers and lives. The well-informed and productive youth of today could be the corner stone for the building of a strong and invincible Democratic society of tomorrow.

Forward

The sun was sparkling in a soft, blue sky. Fluffy white clouds floated lazily by. I took deep breathes of crisp, mountain air as I laid on a freshly mowed lawn and gazed up to drink in the beauty and peacefulness of the day. I was completely at peace and wondered—would it always be like this?

I was barely six years old.

I had completed my chores so I was free to lie on my soft bed of grass and dream.

There was a spark of excitement in me as my dreams led me down my favorite path. I would be going to school come September. I could hardly contain myself as I pondered the wonderful walk to school with my sister Rose and all the big kids. Mom had been working feverishly trying to finish our new school pinafores with the rickrack trim and the pretty white organdy blouses. It was such a good feeling knowing that our hard work in the garden helping Mom and Dad plant, weed and can so many of the vegetables this summer was going to pay off. The money we earned we could buy pencils and maybe even a pencil box! The crayons would come later.

"Teedee—Teedee!"

Well—there it was—Time to go in and set the table. We always helped Mom with supper. Already the tantalizing odors were emanating from the kitchen. Steak sizzling on the stove with the delectable blend of parsley, basil and garlic (those were some of the herbs from our garden) I sure hoped that Mom was making that wonderful lettuce and tomato salad that I loved to soak my bread into when all the salad was gone. The lettuce and tomatoes would be from our garden, too! God—life was good! If there was only some way to make it all stand still—or maybe can it to save it all for later on.

"Teedee-Teedee"!

"I'm coming. I'm coming!"

Chapter I

THE EARLY YEARS

It was 1934—in Pennsylvania—McKean County—in a little village called Hazelhurst, a small place in the world tucked away in the foothills of the Alleghany mountains. I didn't realize it then but life was very difficult. I heard a lot of the grownups talking about a depression. I really didn't understand what that was all about except I did know it had something to do with a lot of folks being out of work. Most of the men in our area worked in the oil fields or in the Quaker State refinery in Farmer's Valley. I used to hear the men talking about walking the pipelines or lay offs at the refinery when they stopped for gas or car repairs at the garage. (My Dad and Uncle Joe owned and ran the garage). The garage was a kind of gathering place for the local gentry. It was a comfortable spot with the gas stove surrounded by the rocking chair and stools—and—oh yes—I can't forget the cuspidor or spittoon as it was commonly called.

I learned a lot of history and geography in those days as I sat quietly listening to the pros and cons of the day. Russia was the terrifying giant that threatened our part of the world. It was fascinating listening to different strategies of how to destroy this terrible threat upon our country. Along with listening to these discussions, I couldn't help counting how many of the fast chewers would miss the spittoon.

The days of summer gradually faded. Autumn appeared with a burst of color that painted the hills and valleys of McKean County into a magical splendor. It was so invigorating and exciting—I was going to school right after Labor Day. Labor Day was always a family fun day. We didn't do anything extravagant or travel any place special because Dad usually had to work at the garage—but it was fun helping Mom prepare a mouth-watering picnic dinner. The smell of her bubbling apple pies was indescribable.

Our job was to set up the table and place the benches around the table in the back yard. In case of rain we would set up the table and chairs on our long ell shaped porch. In any case, this was the one-day Dad got to come home to eat with the family. He would close for a few hours. Other days, Mom would pack a basket with food and we girls would take turns bringing it up to the garage. Mom always packed more food than Dad could eat because there was very often someone in the office with him and he would share the home made bread, pasta, vegetables and dessert with them. No food was ever wasted! This was the 1930's and although to us kids life was great actually it was hard going during these last stages of the depression. Adults talked about the struggle to keep families going with food and other necessities all the time. But it WAS Labor Day and I was going to school for the first time tomorrow! I was so excited I could hardly sleep that night. I had laid out my favorite new pinafore and blouse Mom had made and my new shoes and socks.

There was a lot of hustle and bustle in our house that morning trying to get into the bathroom—we only had one and at that we were fortunate to have a bathtub in it.

Rose was dressed and ready to go first. The table was set with cereal, toast, hot chocolate, and orange juice. We had to sit down to eat something before Mom would let us leave. Rose, being a very obedient child, was sitting eating when I entered the kitchen. I grabbed 2 pieces of toast a swallow of her chocolate and yelled, "Hurry up, Sis, I really want to get there!"

"But Teedee, the first bell hasn't rung yet. After that we still have 15 minutes".

Rose caught up and we were off! Everyone was excited and anxious for the first day. We met Kathy, Ruth and Flora. We all scurried as fast as we could. The playground between the two schoolhouse buildings was filled with anxious and eager kids. Some were on the swings, others on slides—all waiting for that bell to ring. At the sound of the bell we all rushed towards the front of the white building—that was the elementary building. Miss Twila stopped us and told us what room to report to for attendance.

There were 4 very large rooms in the school. The first two housed the 1st and 2nd grades and the 3rd and 4th grades. Upstairs was occupied by the 5th and 6th grade room and the 7th and 8th grade room. It all looked so awesome to me as I entered Room 1.

It was a very big room with large windows on two sides. The room was filled with about forty small desks and chairs. Miss Twila had bright colored pictures all around the room along with large and small case letter charts. In the front of the room was a large, black, round wood stove. This would keep us warm this winter. The chalkboards fascinated me. They covered two sides of the room. In front of one of the black boards was a small semi-circle of little chairs and one large chair. I would find out later that this is where I would learn to read and write.

Chapter II

THE THRILL OF LEARNING

Teedee walked down in the line with the other students and the Patrol guards helped the children cross the busy route 6 that ran through the little village of Hazel Hurst. The garage was busy that day. It was late fall and everyone was hustling to get their cars ready for the usually severe winter days coming soon.

It had already started to snow a fine mist that gradually turned into large wet flakes that clung to everything. That first snowfall was always so thrilling! It seemed to spark life into everyone.

The first chore after school was to stop at the garage to see Dad and Uncle Joe. Sometimes there were little chores that had to be done. Teedee picked up a broom and began to sweep out the office. Mike and Joe were busy checking radiators, batteries, cleaning windshields and pumping gas but it was time to check the mail.

"Teedee, go check the mail", Mike called as he rushed past on his way to get a quart of oil. (Mike was Teedee's father and Uncle Joe and he were partners at the garage). It was fun going to the mail! It was located only a couple of blocks up the street and you had to pass by where all the big kids hung out after school—The Soda Shop!

The Post Office was one of the largest buildings in town. Mr. and Mrs. Larson were the Postmasters and they usually had the mail sorted and ready when Teedee or her sisters came in after school. They also had two sons who helped out once in awhile. All the kids had little jobs and chores to do before supper and then it was on to the homework.

Teedee hurried back after getting the mail and talking to Mrs. Larson. It was beginning to get a little late and it was important to get home to help Mom. There were little jobs to do around the house, especially if Mom had washed clothes. They would be hard to dry out side in the cold weather. Then there was supper to help with—pack the basket with Dad's supper and see that it got up to the garage while it was still warm.

That night after supper when the dishes were done and the kitchen was cleaned and put in order, it was time to practice the piano and do the much-needed homework.

There was a large rectangular dinning room table. There were four girls in the family (Mick wasn't born yet). Each one of the girls had a side of the table to work on.

Rose was two grades ahead and she was busy doing her Math and Reading assignment. Teedee was struggling practicing making her numbers and printing her name. She really hadn't learned to write yet.

It was a cold snowy day just before the holiday season. Winter had settled in quite permanently with tall snow banks created by the plows that worked constantly as the snow continued to fall and drift. It was deer hunting season. That was excitement in itself! Usually the population in the little village of Hazel Hurst doubled during hunting season. Many families "took in" hunters. This was the major way the villagers earned extra holiday money. Down on the farm, that was located on the edge of town, the Houser family always housed at least six or eight hunters and so it went all over town.

The girls were coming back from the garage after delivering Mike's supper and doing a few little jobs for him, when the old church bell began to toll. That was a frightening sound during hunting season. It was a signal that something was wrong. The girls raced home. Shortly after they got there, the little old Ford truck came rather fast and parked out front of the house. Dad walked in. Everyone braced themselves to hear the news.

Dad said, "I have to go down to the cellar to get some extra lights, lanterns and rope that we might need in searching for several lost hunters that haven't returned. I don't know who they all are but they are in Mark Agrossie's hunting party.

Dad urgently collected what he needed and left the house.

As the night wore on more and more lights flickered on the side of the mountain and the church bell began to toll. We girls sat quietly listening to the women as they recalled other times when hunters had been lost on the mountain in the wintertime and those that had disappeared in Catherine's swamp in the summer.

Rose, TeeDee and Melly sat there mesmerized hearing and listening to these stories. "Time for bed", broke the spell and the girls realized it was Mom calling. There was school the next day. This was gospel when we girls were growing up—you NEVER MISSED SCHOOL except for severe illness. Reluctantly, we girls paddled upstairs and prepared for bed. I was lying in a nice warm bed all comfy and cozy. I was wishing that Mark was warm and safe some place, too.

"Oh, Oh", I hadn't finished all my homework on the papers that were due at school in the morning.

I quickly and stealthy pulled out the book that I had put on the dresser with the papers in it. I sat on the top step of the stairs using the book for a desk and began filling in the letters and numbers. I perked up my ears when I heard the women exclaiming something over and over. At first I couldn't figure out what they were saying, but finally I was able to pick up the words "'poor Mark and why did it have to be him?

Tragic accident"!

It was clear to me now. Something terrible had happened to Mark. I didn't feel like finishing those papers. I put them away and crawled under the covers and eventually dozed off.

Morning came quickly and when Mom delivered the news about Mark I felt sick and couldn't really finish eating my breakfast.

On the way to school that morning, the girls talked about how Mark had been shot accidentally. The men with him had tried to get him some help but they had gotten lost. Mark was the only one in the Hunting party that really knew those woods. The others were strangers to the area. Some were from Pittsburgh and the others were from the Philadelphia area. It had taken the town posse half of the night to locate the Hunting party. It was too late for Mark. He'd lost too much blood and they couldn't save him. The others in the party had needed a lot of First Aid. They were half frozen, hungry and devastated over the accident. The girls entered school with heavy hearts.

After opening exercises, which consisted of the pledge of Allegiance to The flag and the "Lord's Prayer", then special intentions, the students with different duties got to work. Leroy went out to bring in the wood for the stove from under the porch of the white building. Ralph set up the little chairs in a circle for Reading, and Ruth passed out papers for the second graders to do their Math. I was with the rest of the first grade students who lined up to take their seats in the Reading circle. This was fun but still a little challenging to some of the students. Miss Twilla took her seat in the group and began with flash cards of letters that formed sounds. This seemed a little bit easier that day and students responded enthusiastically. Next was writing Miss Twilla allowed some of the students who wanted to go up to the blackboard to practice writing letters. I was a little slow at first but then gradually by the end of the week. I began to join the others in the Reading circle to recognize sounds and to put them together to write some of these words on the board. The feeling was exhilarating to actually see a word, know how to say it and know what it meant! Students could hardly wait to get the first "Dick and Jane" books they had been promised when they could recognize most of the vocabulary words. This was the spark that ignited the love of Reading. Later it was called PHONICS.

Chapter III

THE MIDDLE YEARS

The years passed quickly. Each one marked a milestone in Tee-Dee's life and a profound effect of her love of learning. It was in the Second grade that she found out by asking to sit in the front of the room at a desk closest to the chalkboard that she could see better—thus learning quickened it's pace. In the Third grade the world would start to unfold and she became aware of people and places beyond Hazelhurst, McKean county and Pennsylvania. Along with the widening area of knowledge, also came an awareness of civic and social problems.

Danny was a likeable, blue-eyed, freckled faced kid. He sat a couple of seats behind me. His stocky build and bravado act intimidated most of the kids and he seemed to get away with most antics he would dream up to tease the other kids in the class.

It was Friday afternoon and a large social problem loomed before many of the third grade girls who were on the playground during that afternoon recess. IT WAS DANNY! He would lie in wait and as an unsuspecting girl would start going up the stairs to enter the white Building, Danny would grab her and pull her under the closed stairs and try to kiss her!

I started up the stairs and in one grab Danny tried to pull me under the stairs. I reacted quickly and without even thinking. "Darn you, Danny! Get away from me!" I really hit him hard when I had tried to push him away so hard in fact that his nose started to bleed. In his astonishment, I was able to get away. I went storming into the classroom.

Miss Miesel was sitting primly at her desk and raised her glasses on her nose when she heard the racket.

"What is this, Theresa?"

"Danny grabbed me and tried to kiss me and I hit him—hard!"

Danny burst into the room swearing and bleeding profusely from his nose. "I'll get you Teedee for this. You didn't have to hit me, I was only playing with you."

"Come with me Daniel!"

Miss Miesel marched him out of the classroom. I know that I was in for it now! Danny had done it again and would get off easy—I would get most of the blame. I braced myself. Miss Miesel returned to the classroom very stern faced followed by Danny with a smirk on his face and looking very injured. Miss Miesel proceeded to lecture me about hitting any one. She said I should have come in and told her. It was her job to take care of these problems! I tried to explain to her that I had to hit him in order to get away, but she wouldn't even let me finish my sentence. I was furious and most of all, mortified to have her reprimand me that way in front of all my classmates!

That day I ran directly home as fast as I could. I knew Mom would listen and understand! Half way home I remembered that I hadn't taken my Geography book home and I had wanted to finish to read about the Sahara Desert and all the fascinating facts about it—but I was too upset to go back to get it!

Mom did understand. She saw me coming down the walk and left the porch where she was hanging up clothes to meet me.

"Teedee, what is it?"

"Oh, Mom, I'm so darned mad at Danny and Miss Miesel that I just ran home. Now I forgot my books and everything!"

She put her arm around me and said, "Come on we'll talk about it at the kitchen table. I took out of the oven some homemade rolls and pizza. I know that will make you feel better."

As we entered the kitchen, I could smell the freshly baked bread and pizza. It did make me feel better, but I was still very angry!

That year passed with a few more unpleasant incidents but school really was the center of our lives. The subjects that were presented from the third grade to the eighth grade were fascinating. Students were required to memorize, learn through repetition and then in the sixth, seventh and eighth grade, students began to analyze and THINK through processes and to solve problems.

The goal that year was to pass "The Counties"! This was a standardized test made up of three hundred basic questions. Questions were based on all subjects including logic and problem solving. Students were required to obtain a score of ¾ of the questions asked in order to gain entrance into High School. Only several students that year didn't make the grade. The majority of the class passed. I had a score of 290, one of the highest in the class. Needless to say I went home with a big smile and full of chatter about planning the freshman year in High School.

Chapter IV

THE HIGH SCHOOL YEARS—1942

As August "dog days" faded into a glorious colorful September—High School began. It was the most wonderful time of the year! Everything at School had changed. No more White Building with the playground. That was for the little kids. The new scene was the revered and often dreamed about Brick Building. This was the High School. It consisted of four very large rooms. The two on the first floor were for the incoming freshmen. This was the Commercial studies room. By the time I got there, Mrs. Lombard was the teacher who offered subjects for business Training such as Bookkeeping I and II, Shorthand, Business Math and Typing. The desks in this room were all equipped with typewriters—Royals and Underwoods—that were attached into the desks and had to be covered or pulled up to be used. This was wonderful! I was a freshmen and I got to have an assigned seat in this classroom. I knew that these "new" machines fascinated me and this fact influenced my choice of subjects to include Bookkeeping, Typing and Shorthand. I never really entertained the idea of being a Secretary, but I might be able to help my Dad in the office part of the garage.

The other room of the first floor was what we called the Biology room. It was where a Science Lab, equipped with materials to help facilitate the teaching of general Science (all freshmen were required to take) Biology for all sophomores and Chemistry for all juniors and seniors. Health was also taught here and everyone had to take four years of this subject that covered from nutrition to the bone structure and vital organs of the body.

Upstairs one room was devoted to the study of English. This room was stacked with volumes of dictionaries, thesauruses, encyclopedias, magazines, and newspapers. This room I dearly loved because here we learned to transcribe our thought, ideas, and impression on paper. We also were exposed to the composition of our writing and sentence structure. Yes, we diagrammed sentences in order to learn the basic parts and to use these different parts of speech correctly. It was fascinating and I loved it. We wrote poems and stories. Then we read and learned to critic our readings, analyze and listen to the other students' work. There was one thing that stood out in my memory and I carried into my own teaching many years later—that was learning parts of speech and diagramming. We were told that this was our bag of tools to use in writing and repairing our sentences much the same as a mechanic uses his tools to fix an engine to make it run properly.

This room I also remember as the Latin Room. Here I was to study four years of the Latin language. At that time, I didn't realize how important this study was to the basic structure of the English language, and also a good background to the study of ancient History. Later I discovered it also helped me to understand my religion. Being Catholic, I learned to follow the Mass, then always said in Latin. When I joined the choir later, it helped me to learn to sing the Latin hymns and the Requiem Masses. This activity filled a great part of my younger years and the effect has remained with me for a lifetime.

The last room upstairs in the Brick Building was the room that intrigued me the most. The History Room was where we were taught Ancient History and U.S. History and civics. Civics and Government was taught to all students from incoming freshmen to seniors. Civics and Government were essential—then came U.S. History divided into two phases—early Colonial period to the Civil War followed by the Civil War to World War II. This was really interesting because we had most of our information on World War II first hand. It came from the radio, newspapers, movies, magazines, and newsreels at the movies. All this news hadn't had a chance to be compiled and written into a textbook. This gave us a good opportunity to be able to distinguish fact from propaganda. Great emphasis was placed on this concept. It really touched home because there wasn't anyone who wasn't affected some way or another by this horrible war. Both close and distant relatives of almost everyone were involved. Stories and atrocities were filmed in sometime very graphic ways and were presented in Life magazine, different periodicals and especially in the famous Newsreels that exploded all over this country.

I remember vividly the day the letter came from Johnsonburg, my mother's hometown, that our cousin, Joe, who had been a Turret Gunner in an airplane had been gunned down in an air raid. Mom was devastated. She had helped to care for him as a baby as well as some of the older children in the family. She was especially fond of her uncle who had helped to raise her after her father's death. So it had hit close to home and we all grieved.

Cousins and friends' names began to appear daily in the newspapers as casualties in the Army, Marines, Navy, and Air Force began to filter in. Everything and everyone was geared towards the war. We were living in a time when history was being made. Our teachers alerted us to this fact. Rumors of a Holocaust began to come into the news and there arose big doubts about these stories. Was it fact or indeed propaganda? All we did was to study these facts until later the real stories began to unfold in the later days of the war and after the war was over.

Again, it was probably this series of events that prompted me to begin to formulate the career path I was to follow for most of my life. We really didn't have Guidance Counselors to help us with career choices. We did take aptitude tests. These tests gave our teachers some indication in directing us to choose the subjects that we would succeed in the most. Therefore, a greater part of my time in this classroom was devoted to history and Geography rather than Math courses, Problem solving, and one year of Algebra, but to take Trig or Calculus was an option.

The freshman year for the most part flew by with great movie and great songs dominating the Hit Parade. Frank Sinatra was everybody's idol along with the great actors and actresses in Hollywood. I really didn't get to see too many of these great movies until I got to college, but playing the piano and having to pay only 35 cents a copy for most of the popular sheet music, I gathered most of the music of the day. My favorites then and still are, "Embraceable You", "All or Nothing at All", "Blue Moon", and Kate Smith's version of "God Bless America".

That first year in high school we were encouraged to fill every minute of our school day with courses, study and extra curricular activities. I dived into all of it. I studied piano, joined the band as Drum Major, became writer and editor of the school paper, sang in musicals, painted the scenery for musicals and plays, decorated and helped plan major school events, proms, parties and school dances.

As I look back now, the only thing our school courses lacked in our little country schoolhouse was physical education training. There were no specified phys ed. classes in high school. Unless you played softball, bowled, swam, roller-skated or ice-skated on your own there was no activity provided in the school curriculum.

There was always plenty of exercise around. The daily chores that all young people were expected to do and did do on a regular basis. When chores were finished the younger crowd went sledding, ice-skating or skiing in the winter months. The other seasons of the year were filled with swimming, baseball, tag and walking the trails in the woods and around town. Yard games were very popular. Croquet was a "biggy" along with badminton and tennis.

As the years progressed, I became entrenched in the school schedule and discovered a wide variety of personalities and friends. Because of the intensity of the war going on, many of these friends—one by one—left to join the different branches of service. It was a sad day when the friends that she had been attracted to left to join the marine Corps; Bob, Frank, Carmen, O'Neil, Eddie and Bill. Some were older and had already finished school. Then a few started to leave school as the war intensified. It was an exhilarating, happy and sad time all at once.

The sophomore year for most students left in school was pretty uneventful except a new music teacher landed in town and caused a ripple in the everyday routine life. Teenie was a very attractive and spirited personality. She seemed to fit in and become a favorite to all age groups in town. She was kind of a free spirit and livened things up considerably. Some of the traditional school board members looked at her with raised eyebrows at times but not me. She became another major influence in my life—music and teaching. Teachers can become very influential to students and can serve as a role model and in many cases making school classrooms so interesting and enjoyable that students will be encouraged to stay in school. That year was packed with a variety of musical and social activities along with a ridged scholastic schedule. The curriculum was strictly academic—little or no frills. It consisted of Biology, Latin I or II, English, Ancient History, Civics, Math, Typing, Shorthand and Bookkeeping.

By the time that the junior year rolled around, the war had intensified and many students left to join the service. My class was forced to have its prom in the middle of the school year. This presented many problems. In order to do a good job it required a lot of planning, since the committee had to look out of town for an adequate place to hold the dinner and dance. It was the middle of the winter and snowplows had already been working overtime trying to keep up with the snow falling. In spite of the weather and other difficulties, Mrs. Lombard with her eager student committee set out to order the dinner menu and decorate the hotel ballroom in Kane, a distance of fifteen miles away, into a winter wonderland for the prom.

The exciting night finally arrived. Luckily it had not snowed that day and everyone who was going with Mr. & Mrs. Lombard was to meet at my father's garage.

My father was talking seriously to Mr. Lombard. "Remember now—not too late. The snow has held off but it is supposed to start again sometime tonight. These roads will be impassible if much more comes down."

Mr. Lombard agreed with my father and promised to get everyone home safe and sound.

The little party left in gay spirits and headed for Kane and the prom. It was an exciting affair—everything looked so festive and truly it was a fairy winter wonderland. After everyone had arrived, Mrs. Lombard led the lively crowd into the dining room. A tempting and delicious complete roast beef dinner was served with everyone's favorite dessert and the happy students then adjourned into the ballroom. The Big Band Sound Orchestra played all the popular songs of the day—"Embraceable You", "Blue Moon", "Sunrise Serenade", "My Buddy" and of course all the popular jitterbug numbers. Everyone seemed to be having a blast. Twelve o'clock approached so quickly that no one even thought to check outside. While a delirious good time was enjoyed inside, outside had become a literal white out. It had been snowing with a howling wind whipping the snow into unbelievable huge snow banks since nine o'clock. No one had any idea that all transportation and all means of communication had been cut off. Telephone lines were down. Everything had come to a literal stand still. Only the howling wind and the white piles of snow seemed to dominate our part of the world.

The chaperones were panicked, especially Mr. Lombard. He had promised to get us all home safely. With road that were closed and impassible and no buses running, this was going to be an impossible task. He would at least try to use the telephone to alert parents of the situation. "Oh, no"! Telephone lines to Hazel Hurst were down. No communication!

The hotel manager came out into the lobby and offered everyone to stay there in the lobby. He provided an ample supply of refreshments and hot beverages to the kids and band members. It was like a big all night party—or so it seemed to the kids. But not to the chaperones who were concerned about how they were going to get everyone home safely. At four o'clock in the morning, most of the kids had found comfortable nooks and corners and had curled up and begun to doze off. The excitement and the adventure of the day had begun to take its toll.

Sun streamed in and glistened on the newly fallen snow that had been piled up by the wind and the all night plows. Groggy students and weary chaperones stirred as the hotel manager spoke to Mr. Lombard. He gathered everyone around him and announced that arrangements had been made with a Greyhound Bus to transport all of us to Napolitan's Service Station in Hazel Hurst. From there Mr. Lombard said, "Parents will be notified to pick up students."

That was going to be tricky because a lot of the family cars were still buried in the snow in Kane. Just a few of the boys had driven family cars to the prom, but first things first. And that meant getting home.

It was a scary ride early that morning even in a large bus. A small path had been cleared in the middle of a two-way road. Only a very few commercial vehicles had to share the roadway. Once or twice the bus began to slide and everyone held their breath until the bus with a sudden lurch was stopped by one of the huge snow banks that lined the highway. With our hearts in our mouths, the bus finally pulled into the service station. That was the longest fifteen miles I ever traveled! Dad was there to greet us. He didn't look like a happy camper. It was a tremendous relief to get off that bus! All I wanted to do was to get out of these clothes and take a nice warm bath to relax and crawl into a soft, warm bed!

Although there was a look of relief, the sternness in my dad's face did not relax. He looked at me and said, "Teedee, there is a path shoveled on the side of the road. Use it to get home and remember there's school today and I expect you to be there at nine o'clock!"

I was devastated!

How could I get home, change and get ready in time to go to school? Well, it would have to be worked out. This was the thinking of the day. Most parents' major concern was to see to it that their children were sent to school and expected to learn. Parents also saw to it that homework was done and school projects were completed. After family, school was the number one priority and that was the way it was carried out. As a result, school incidents, student rebellion and truancy were at a minimum. It was a productive time for both students and parents.

As the year rolled on, the war became more and more a part of people's lives. Classes in school continued to diminish—boys especially were signing up for active duty. Girls and women felt they too had to join in the war effort.

During that summer, a few of the girls in my class got jobs working in the local factories. I, with my sister Rose, went to Erie, Pennsylvania to our Uncle Nick's. A problem had come up in the family. One of Nick's children had asthma and needed some country fresh air for a few months. So Mom and her brother Nick decided to send Donny and Marie to live in Hazel Hurst for the summer. Then Rose and I would go to Erie with Uncle Nick and Aunt Vi. This was great news for us. Now I decided this was my big opportunity. I would fudge my age—at sixteen I looked more like eighteen anyway. Well, it was worth a try!

Chapter V

THE WAR EFFORT AND THE BIG CITY

Living in the city in 1945 was an education in itself. There were several important issues that flared at this time in the Erie, but in most bigger cities in the Northeast.

The one that struck me the most was one that I was completely ignorant about—Racism. Growing up in a small isolated village most people were not faced with this problem. We rarely or hardly ever saw a person of color. When I first boarded a bus to go home after applying at Zern's for a war time job, I was shocked to see an elderly black woman board the bus carrying a heavy package and no one got up to give her a seat. I looked around and immediately got up and offered her the seat. She was a little reluctant at first, but I insisted and she quietly sat down with a look of relief and disbelief on her face.

I really didn't know or understand the hostile looks I got on the bus that day until I got home and Uncle Nick approached me. He just happened to be seated in the back of the bus and witnessed my giving up my seat and the reaction of people sitting around him. He tried to explain why this was a dangerous thing to do and how it could cause real trouble.

I was shocked and asked, "How can people be so disrespectful and cruel to an older person?"

"I don't know, Teedee, but that's the way it is and you shouldn't put yourself in the middle that way".

Being a spirited young girl and an independent thinker, I did not accept his explanation. I had learned to listen to different points of view, but I had

30

also learned to express my views in a Civics Debating class in High School. I proceeded to say what I thought.

"All due respect, Uncle, I don't see it that way. And maybe someday other people will see it my way, too. People deserve to be treated for who they are. Neither color, race nor religion should make a difference."

"O.K. kid, I just hope you don't learn the hard way."

After a couple of weeks, I got my routine down so that I began to learn the city streets and my way to work in the morning—or so I thought—

I left the bus and stepped onto the street to the factory. I only had a couple of blocks to go when I became conscience of a large white car (could have been some kind of a limo) that was approaching from behind me and it kept slowing down. I could feel the goose bumps starting to form and the prickly feeling at the nape of my neck—I was scared!

The car pulled up to the curb and cut off my crossing path. Before I could decide what to do, three black young men that had been walking every day to the factory at the same time that I was stepped between me, and the car. The driver quickly changed his mind and sped away. Joe, Moe and Dane saved me that morning and I was forever grateful to them and decided I would seek their company walking to work every morning.

Besides broadening my outlook on the world around me I also learned a very valuable lesson that summer that changed my life and stayed with me to shape my future days. For a kid, I was making "big bucks" both from working a full shift in the defense factory and the tips plus wages that I received working at the restaurant. But I knew then this was not the life I would want to pursue. I loved school and I knew I would set my goal into pursuing a career in the education field.

That summer taught me some very valuable lessons about life and people.

For instance—one day in the factory when I was struggling to keep the conveyor belt running, I met a pleasant girl who seemed to know a lot about repairing the belt and who seemed to have a happy, humorous personality. Her name, I discovered later, was Bernice and everyone seemed to like her and called her Bernie. She became an everyday experience that I looked forward to working with and talking to.

One afternoon as Bernie and I were finishing up a job on the conveyor belt in Compartment 24, she asked me if I would join her at a small gathering with her friends on the west side of town.

I replied, "Gosh, Bernie, I'll have to check this with my Uncle and if he thinks it's O.K. I'll see you there. Give me that address, just in case."

This really was going to be my first real social adventure on my own. All summer I had been spending all my time working eight hours in the factory and four to five hours at the restaurant. This was an exciting, new experience for me. I looked forward to doing something social.

When I got home I enthusiastically approached my Uncle Nick and asked him if he approved of my taking an evening off from his friend's restaurant to go to this party at another restaurant on the west side of town with my friend Bernie. After a barrage of questions and inquiries, he reluctantly said O.K.—but to be home by 10 o'clock. He also went over the bus route with me and said he would be at the last bus stop to walk me the rest of the way home.

This sounded good to me!

I quickly showered and picked out my newest peasant skirt and blouse (that's what they were wearing that summer), I slipped into my new sandals that matched my outfit—fixed my page boy hair style and thinking I was the "cats meow" left our house on my new adventure.

After boarding the bus on Van Buren Avenue, I excitedly watched as the streets passed by and before I knew it, we were at the first stop where I had to get a transfer ticket. I quickly boarded the bus that was to take me to my destination—Alberto's Restaurant. As the bus pulled in there standing waiting for me was my friend Bernie.

She wasn't all dressed up like I thought she would be. This struck me as rather odd. She was still wearing the same mannish clothes that she had worn to work on the conveyor belt. "Oh well, maybe she just didn't have time to change into something more dressy."

"Hi Bernie, all set for some good lasagna and good music?"

"Yeah, you bet."

"Where are the others? Inside or couldn't Della and Joan make it?"

"I'll tell you when we get inside. Come on I've reserved us a table."

The restaurant was very attractive—typically Italian décor with the red, white, and green colors—but best of all was the scrumptious orders emanating from the kitchen." So far, so good. But why was I not feeling comfortable?

The meal lived up to the great reputation of the restaurant in every way—on the dance floor people began to filter out in response to the music being played by the orchestra. A couple of nice looking young men were eyeing our table and finally one of them got up and came over and asked if they could buy us a drink. I said I would enjoy a soft drink but Bernie asked for a scotch and soda. He motioned for the other one to join our table. Al and Bob were lots of fun—kept us laughing and amused until I felt a little more relaxed. Then Al asked me to dance. I was delighted because there was nothing more that I like to do than dance especially on the faster numbers like the Jitterbug.

When we returned from the dance floor Bob had gone and Bernie sat there looking a trifle uncomfortable. The aura of gaiety had slipped away and Al asked if he could see me again some time. I said I'd let him know and he left.

Bernie asked me to go into an empty room beside the restaurant where the girls usually met. I hesitated—but then out of curiosity decided to go in. As we approached the room, Bernie put her arm around me and I took it as a friendly gesture—but when we were in the room she tried to kiss me—I was shocked, startled and confused—I knew instinctively I had to get out of there fast. With one good push I ducked out of her reach and raced for the door. Not stopping for anything, I ran down the block to catch my first bus home. I got home at

9:30 and my Uncle was there to meet me and he walked me home. Of course they were anxious to know all about my good time.

"Well, how was your night out?" my Uncle asked, "and how come you came back so early?"

Still in a state of confusion and not really understanding the implication of Bernie's actions, I simply answered, "I didn't like the company, so I came home."

It was a long time after that that I fully understood about Bernie.

Being away from home at the age of sixteen proved to be an exciting and sometimes dangerous experience. Later as I looked back, I was glad that I had a good Aunt and Uncle who guided me through much of that summer adventure.

It was Sunday morning and one of the neighbor's boys who lived two houses down the street came over.

"Hey, Teedee, do you want to go for a ride with me on my new motorcycle?"

"Gosh, Ted, I don't know. I've never really ridden on a motorcycle before!"

"Well, wait and I'll ask my Uncle if it would be O.K."

"Uncle Nick, Can I take a ride on Ted's new bike?"

"Not until I go first," he replied.

"O.K., I'll wait until you come back—this should be fun!"

I waited impatiently until they came back. I was a little bit apprehensive when they came roaring back up the driveway—but I wasn't about to let them know.

With full bravado, I hopped on the bike behind Ted and we roared off. I had to admit, it was exhilarating and fun as long as I could hang on tight to Ted. But then my fears were realized as he hit a curb going around a corner and we were thrown from the bike onto the grass. Good thing he had slowed down considerably to take the corner. We ended up with some pretty good bruises and scratches and I decided right then and there—motorcycle riding was not my cup of tea!

I learned a lot of lessons that summer—I decided I really wanted to finish high school and go on to college. So my future was beginning to take shape.

Chapter VI

LAST YEAR AT HOME

That summer proved to be one of the most stressful and emotional ones of my entire life.

Mom, unaware to us and I believe even to her except for the last few months, was pregnant and expecting the baby around the first few weeks of May. There was all that extra end of the year activity plus standard achievement tests that we had to take. It was from these scores that the Principal (with no guidance Councilors in our little country school) would interview each of us and advise us on our future careers. So we all felt the necessity to bone up on the basics to attain the highest possible score, especially those of us that wished to attend college.

Besides our specific chores to do at home and helping Dad at the garage, these new duties loomed over us. We realized that we would have to take over the entire household these last few weeks before Mom would go to the hospital. In addition to all of this, we were worried about Mom. She had not been doing so well these past few weeks and frankly we were selfishly scared we might lose her. To teenagers, this situation seemed almost insurmountable.

The dreaded day finally arrived. Of course it was early in the morning about four or five o'clock and we heard Dad bustling about getting ready to take Mom to the hospital. We all got up and busied ourselves with all the morning chores. Thank goodness it wasn't a school day! In fact, it was Mother's Day, May 12, 1946. Can you imagine—on Mother's Day? The first blow struck my heart. Here it was our day to be with Mom and we couldn't be. We had to stay home to take care of things. We were in tears and praying that God would take care of her so she could come back home to us. All the animosity that we had harbored all these past months disappeared. All I could think was—"Mom please get through this so we can have you home again."

That day was so long but as the shadows of evening began to take shape, Dad came with the exciting news that all had gone well with Mom and that we had a new baby brother.

"When can we see her?"

"I'll take you tomorrow after school to see Mom and Michael, Jr.", Dad said with a big grin.

Right after school Dad got the old Packard out and we were off.

The Kane Community Hospital was about twenty to twenty-five minutes away. As we approached the hospital the realization set in that my life was about to change dramatically again.

There was Mom—pale and very weak looking but smiling and when I set eyes on my baby brother all fears and selfishness about my Mom's being pregnant vanished. I loved that little pumpkin and decided right then and there this would be my summer goal—to help Mom with the baby.

I remember as Mom was recuperating, that I got the first look of recognition from Mick and then saw his first steps. He loved Ritz crackers and I was guilty of indulging him on his first food calories. He was a joy and I was rewarded by one of his first words—"Tee Yee"!

It was time to pack and get ready for college. I was apprehensive because our principal at the high school had cautioned me about my only weakness in academics could be English. I was shaken by his input because I thought I had a pretty good grasp of that subject. I determined right then and there to work to make English my best subject.

We loaded the Packard up with all my gear—which included two suitcases and a box of goodies Mom had insisted we take and I was off to college.

Chapter VII

THE COLLEGE YEARS 1946-1950

I kept thinking when we arrived at Mansfield College's beautiful campus that I was going to be a teacher! I was thrilled at the prospect but apprehensive of what it was going to take to complete the courses. It was an exciting day. Mom and Dad helped unload my suitcases and after checking in and getting the room assignment, we took the elevator to the third floor and entered what was to be my home for the next year.

The family left after an hour or so and I had received word that my roommate Vonnie would not be arriving until much later in the week. So I prepared to settle my things and read over the pamphlet I had gotten at the registration desk. The next day would be Orientation Day for the rules and regulations for incoming Freshmen in the morning. That afternoon we would work out the schedule for the subjects we would be required to take according to our majors—also we would be assigned a professor who would be our guidance person and advisor.

It was a busy and exhilarating time. I could hardly get to sleep anticipating all that would be happening in the days to come. Orientation lasted about an hour right after breakfast. Breakfast was neat. We were all assigned to round tables in the large cafeteria. Each table had an oversized pitcher of milk and one of orange juice. We had a choice of bacon or sausage, toast, French toast, scrambled eggs, butter, jam and coffee. Each week we got assigned to different tables and this enabled students to get acquainted with the different students in the school.

A lot of the students in those first few weeks of school got homesick and freshmen were not allowed or given permission to go home until after the first six weeks when grades would come out. If grades were above a C you then, with written permission from home, could sign out for a weekend home, providing you didn't have classes scheduled on Saturday, which many freshmen did.

The Student Center, which was located right adjacent to North Hall, the girls' dorm where I was assigned and where segments of the Freshmen class were to report. Here schedules for the first semester were to be filled out.

My schedule was mostly the basic required subjects with choices of one or two electives. All freshmen were required to take English, Psychology, History, Physical Education and then the basic requirements for whatever department you were in. for Music, it would have been Solfeggio, Ear Training, Piano, Voice, Beginner Band and Orchestra plus the basic academics. It was a pretty heavy load and it kept freshmen so busy that most of the students didn't have time for much of anything else.

It wasn't until after six weeks or so when students were organized and feeling a little more secure in their routine that they had time to think about their social life.

Student dances, various programs, and different varieties of entertainments were sponsored by the Student Council (made up of upper classmen) every Friday evening from six to ten. Freshmen were limited because they had to be in their rooms by seven o'clock and lights out by ten o'clock. If grades were kept up and with parents' written consent, freshmen were given a little more freedom on weekends.

It was 1946. Many of the students were much older than the seventeen to eighteen year-olds that year. They were the men and women that had returned from the different branches of the service after World War II. These older men and women were entitled to an education and the books necessary to complete their courses.

It was surprising how these older students blended in so well and really added so much to classes and to help advise the younger students. The knowledge and experience they brought to the classrooms was invaluable.

I was one of the young Freshmen students that received help and advice from a group of these veterans. Some of the younger classmen—Eddie, Moe, Jeannie, Phyllis, Melly and I formed a Study Buddy club especially for Psychology classes and later were joined by Joey, Bruce, Jimmy, Nello and Jake who became the instructor. Jake was a brain with a photogenic mind and he was able to condense all the important information that we were supposed to master from the content of the reading, notes, or lectures in class.

It was great fun, too! We all looked forward to meeting after classes. We had two favorite spots. One was the Dairy Store—over Cokes, cheeseburgers, fries or sodas. Jake would drill us on the main ideas or basic points of the lesson. This was serious business. We all had to be able to define all terminology used in the lesson, pick out and discuss major concepts and then defend our positions.

Schooling in the late forties and early fifties was mostly classic, traditional basic subjects. Along with all basic subjects that were mandatory in all curriculum areas, Industrial Arts, Home Economics, Music, Swimming, Archery, Tennis, Physical Education were considered the popular electives. This kept most college students very busy along with library assignment readings that were required for most classes. Students learned to organize their schedules to cover all necessary work, classes and assignments so that they could enjoy a reasonable amount of leisure time for the most important social activities on and off campus. There were also many extra curricular areas offered to students. Most popular ones providing a variety of activities and general excitement were the Sports teams: Football, Baseball, Bowling and Tennis.

That fall the excitement grew when Parents' Day was scheduled in early October. The marching band had been practicing, the football team was hard at work perfecting their plays and strategies, students scrambled to get all assignments done to have enough free time to enjoy all the activities planned by the Student Council for that weekend. Finally the night came before the big football game on Saturday. After the game a reception for all parents was held with a special dinner in the Dining Room in North Hall. Many of the parents left after dinner to return home. Girls, including me, rushed up to our rooms to dress for the big dance that evening.

I had only been out with Bill several times to the movies and the Dairy Store and wondered what a really big date would be like. After showering I donned the beautiful rose gown that Mom had made and brought with her that day. With jewelry to match and my carefully combed hair into a stylish pageboy, I felt sparkling and that is exactly what the evening turned out to be—"sparkling". Bill was perfect! He was an excellent dancer, popular with everyone, because he was on the football team and best of all he was a perfect gentleman! When he left me at the dorm door, he even asked me is he could kiss me good night. I was thrilled and walked into the dorm feeling like a fairy princess.

As time went on that year, I learned much about life as well as the enlightenment of education. I learned the hard way sometimes that it was necessary to adhere to rules and regulation if you wished to be successful. One of the lessons I learned the hard way was when girls were off campus during the school week, they had to be inside the building at ten o'clock sharp. The bell would toll loud and clear at ten o'clock and the guards would be locking all entrance doors to the girls' dorm.

It was Friday night and I had feverishly finished all my research at the Library and had all the important material to use in writing my science paper and I looked forward to meeting Carm to go to the movies. I did so want to see "Gone With the Wind" and he had asked me to go. It was a wonderful movie and I cried at the end because we were sort of sad about the ending. Carm suggested we stop and have a hot fudge sundae before going back to the dorm. I glanced at my watch and realized it was cutting the time a little short. But because the magic of the evening hadn't really worn off temptation won out. We had our hot fudge sundae thoroughly enjoying every minute of it—when I froze—the ten o'clock bell began to toll. We raced out of the Dairy Store, which was about five minutes off campus and raced towards North Hall reaching the dorm after the doors were locked.

Carm said, "Don't worry, I'll get a guard on his rounds to open the door to let you in."

He did. But I felt so guilty that I went directly to the Dean of Women, Miss Wasley's room. I knocked and Miss Wasley responded. "Why, what is it Theresa? You look so upset?"

My heart was pounding as I entered her room and began to pour out my story. I said we had been at the movies—I had wanted to see "Gone With the Wind" and that Carmen had offered to take me. It was a long movie—but instead of going right back to the dorm, we had gone to the Dairy Store. By the time I had gotten to the dorm the doors were locked and Carm had to find a guard to let me in.

There was a long moment of silence. I shuttered. In my mind in that long, horrible moment I could feature my disappointed Mom and furious father coming down to pick me up to take me home. I was devastated. To my astonishment, Miss Wasley came over and patted my hand and spoke these astonishing words, "You were truthful and reported yourself to me and that is remarkable. Although you will have to go before the Student Council for this misdemeanor, they will probably rule no offense because you were truthful and didn't try to excuse yourself by sneaking in and that will be my decision, too."

She continued, "Now go to your room and get a good night's sleep and don't worry!"

I can't explain the relief I felt as I left her room and walked down the hall through the foyer to my room.

I made many mistakes that first year in college. I knew I had a lot to learn. But I knew one thing. I loved to learn and I loved training to teach. I had to admit that my father had been right when he steered me towards this profession. When we had talked about careers and the future, I had always expressed a deep desire to study medicine or journalism. But being a foreign, old-fashioned father, he did not approve of girls in those professions. So he had successfully talked me out of it and into the teaching profession—especially since he was footing the basic bills. Mom was a little more understanding.

I did manage to carry good grades, an active campus social life and work at several jobs to augment my spending money in addition to what my father had provided.

Going back to school the autumn of my Junior year was a memorable one. Mother had made me a stylish brown wrap around crepe skirt and a brown silk blouse. It was a chocolate brown and I had brown suede pumps and handbag to match. That year, I returned to school by bus. Dad had been busy at the garage and the Greyhound bus came right by the garage on Route 6. Dad would step out and flag it down for several of us returning to school. I had help with my several suitcases and it was convenient.

In those days, 1947-1948, college students usually traveled light and did not have the convenience items that require a truck or U-Haul to take them back to school and to settle into their dorm rooms. About the only tool some students had was a portable typewriter. All other study items were at school, which included: pencils, pens, notebooks, and an excellent Library. Books were bought at the bookstore with all the other necessary materials. Hours were spent in the Library researching materials for class, required reading and papers due.

The bus conveniently pulled right up into the driveway between North Hall and the Student Center. Several people were there to greet some of the students and I also noticed a photographer who was walking towards me. I realized at once that I was selected for an interview with the area newspaper. He took several pictures of me with my luggage and I answered a few questions about returning to school that year and what my expectations were for that year.

I noticed a young man in the crowd that had gathered. He was with a few of my friends. I decided right then and there I would ask Ed who he was. Little did I realize, that he would be the center of my romantic interests for my remaining days of college.

I tried not to seem too interested when I met him finally at the Dairy Store. I was working there then on my hours off between classes several days a week. He came in with Bruce and Ed. When I waited on the booth—the boys gave me a hard time—teasing me but finally they introduced me to Glenn.

I knew then that I would never forget the twinkling in those blue-green eyes and those heavy eyebrows that seemed to draw me like a magnet. I was nonchalant, as cool as I could be, and unruffled by their antics—my pounding heart!

The next day he showed up in my science class and I hated to admit it, but I was delighted. He had a wonderful sense of humor and he was sort of mysterious in little funny ways of speaking and acting. I was definitely attracted to him—but I was also determined that he was not going to deter me from my goal of finishing my education to become a teacher.

I did live through a lot of heartaches because of this commitment to myself. Socially, I had a good time. If it was not with the Study Buddy group it was with the fellas and gals that I met in my classes. It was the Big Band era of the 40's and 50's and many of the bands came to perform in Elmira. This was a big date and all the girls vied to be asked to go. Girls didn't have cars on campus—the boys did—most of them being GI's. With written permission from parents, the girls were permitted to go with a twelve o'clock curfew. At the stroke of twelve, girls had to be inside the dorm.

It was an interesting post war period. The United States was shifting gears to get back into a normal economy. Schools were breaking ground into new and expanding curriculum especially in Science and Math. The atomic bomb designed by a physicist, Enrico Fermi, produced the first nuclear chain reaction in 1942. This led to a whole new world of developments that were to change our world forever. On October 4, 1957, the Russians launched Sputnik I, man's first artificial satellite followed by Sputnik II in November of that same year. The United States followed shortly after in that next year with the satellite Explorer I on January 31, 1958. The world stage was being set for more and greater strides that would affect our changing world.

But our public schools were slow to keep pace with a changing world. Curriculums began to expand slightly to meet the needs of the various foreign students that began to fill our classrooms also the subject of segregation began to creep into consideration for school authorities.

Public schools began to flourish in the 1930's. The big change was that they organized state systems of public schools that would be open equally and freely to all. Public schools not only taught reading, writing and arithmetic, but also included courses in Arts, bookkeeping, drawing, geography, history, homemaking, manual training, music, nature study, physical education and science. Most students learned readily—not all at the same pace or the same degree—but at least most could master the basics—reading, writing and math.

More and more foreign-born students filled the classrooms. Early on—provisions were made in schools to meet this challenge. English as a second language (ESL) classes were formed to help students make the needed transition from native languages to English. In the early 40's and 50's students seemed to be able to make this transition in three to four years or some even sooner. Public school life seemed to meet requirements and students seemed to learn. This was accomplished because most parents and students viewed school as top priority. Parents cooperated with schools and took a deep interest in helping (if they were able) or seeing that required homework was completed.

Students also had responsibilities to carry out for their parents. Out in the rural sections where larger consolidated schools were built, students arrived home in time to do chores on the farm. Many students took care of livestock, planting in the spring and harvesting in the fall. Family life was important and the local schools became centers of activity and recreation for the whole family.

My college years were fast coming to a close. In order to include all the courses that I felt were necessary to have, I had completed two majors in Social Studies and English and a minor in Music.

In May 1950, Mom and Dad with little Mickey came to see me graduate. I remember what a bittersweet day that was. I had gotten a few awards for journalism, as editor of the college newspaper, working on the yearbook and being on Dean's list in my Junior and Senior years. There was one outstanding proud moment that day I remember, after I received my diploma, and when I went to meet my parents, I saw that they were talking with the Dean of women. Later, I found out that she was complementing me for my ambition, hard-working efforts as a student, and especially my behavior as a college student.

I was not able to go home with my parents that day and this made up the bitter part of the day. I had signed up to go to the Poconos to work as a governess for three children for the Arnet family. They were just starting a Resort complex. Some building was still going on and when the dining area was completed I was to train as a waitress in the Dining Room—Nightclub area.

I said good-bye to my parents and slowly walked down to the Dairy Store to board the Greyhound bus that would be stopping there. I realized then that my girlhood life had come to an end—Now I would be facing the adult world. I also mused while riding on the bus that my pet nickname "Teedy" had to go too. From now on, I would be called Terry instead.

The bus stopped at Strausberg station and I grabbed my suitcase and left the bus. Looking anxiously around I saw Mr. Arnet and he quickly decided that I was the girl who had signed up for the job.

It was a short ride from Strausberg through the Pocanos to Fernwood. Once there all my fears evaporated into thin air. The people were warm and friendly. I met the three children that I would be caring for while their family put the finishing touches on the Resort and restaurant before it would officially open.

It was an entirely new world that surrounded me. The children were delightful and I enjoyed caring for them while the rest of the family was busy preparing the new Resort. It took just a few weeks before the dining room and nightclub area would be finished. The excitement mounted each day. I was kept plenty busy with the children all day and then took dining room orientation instruction in the evening. There was so much to learn about the menu, both food and beverages, as well as how to order from the kitchen. This really was an experience. I learned more about a side of life that I never imagined existed.

The cooks were mostly all derelicts who had suffered great personal tragedies and had become alcoholics. Because of these circumstances they had become homeless people living in Skid Row in New York City. Most of these men had once been career people—doctors, lawyers, accountants, business executives and others had good worthwhile jobs but personal tragedy had become so overwhelming that they gave way to alcoholism.

The men were excellent cooks but they were extremely volatile and were capable of waging war in the kitchen. We learned early on not to return an order to the kitchen if a customer was dissatisfied for any reason—better put in a whole new order and give the cooks plenty of praise.

This became a school of hard knocks—learning to deal with the many different customers, the cooks, learning the menus and working with other people necessary to run the nightclub restaurant for the Resort. But it was all worth it for two very good reasons. One, the management was wonderful. And secondly, they treated you as an individual and made sure that nobody mistreated you or took advantage of the young people that they employed. It was a worthwhile learning experience with hands on training and the young country girl from Pennsylvania began to see what the other side of life was all about.

The summer passed quickly and soon it was time to return home and prepare for my first teaching job.

Chapter VIII

FIRST YEARS OF TEACHING 1950-1953

It was a great time to be in school teaching especially in a New York state consolidated school. Savonna Central School was in the center of a farming community. The students came from the small towns surrounding Savonna and many students came from the dairy and potato farms located in the area.

My first assignment was teaching three English classes in the high school, two classes of Social Studies to Juniors and Seniors, and one period in the Library. I also had the assignment of coaching the senior play. The other responsibility was tutoring students who were to take N.Y. State Regents test in the spring of the school year. This meant that three nights a week I was at the school helping students prepare for this exam. The other two school nights from seven to nine-thirty the assignment was to help out with various responsibilities for the basketball team. This was the heart and center of the community recreation for everyone, children and adults alike. Great competition flourished between Savonna, Campbell and the surrounding town's high school teams. It was great fun and everyone enjoyed the camaraderie and good sportsmanship that was fostered by these games. It also provided an excellent way for teachers to get to know parents, students, and their families better.

When I finished my day at school, I had to run home to teach several piano students. Melly, who taught in the elementary grades, took on the task of cooking dinner for us and three other teachers who roomed in the same house that we were in. It made for an interesting day. Melly was a really good cook so we all enjoyed ourselves—not only for the good food, but also sharing the events of the school day.

Gradually, as the year went on, teachers began to get their classes and extra curricular activities under control. Homeroom teachers had to keep attendance record books. These were not simple. Besides recording attendance for each students enrolled in the homeroom, the percentage of attendance also had to be figured. Each column of figures had to balance out with the totals. Sometimes this would require a whole evening to get it to balance correctly. They were collected and checked each month.

Teaching classes was the best. Students were dedicated to learn. Parent interest and attitude towards students learning, homework and student behaviors helped both student and teachers maintain an excellent classroom environment.

Basic curriculum core subjects were taught. English, History, Geography, Math, and Science with Home economics, Shop (as it was referred to then), Music, Art and Physical Education was taught on different levels for different grades.

There was a gym, athletic field, playground and a cafeteria. This was essential because many students were bussed in from the surrounding farms. Teachers had bus duty, playground duty on rotating schedules and the high school teachers had after school and evening activities that they were assigned to do. It was a heavy, busy, schedule but because of the excellent attitude of most of the parents and students it was not only satisfying, but also enjoyable. There was very little discontent among teachers or students. If a problem emerged, it was dealt with swiftly and fairly.

The attendance was very good and drop out rate at the high school was very low. Not much time was devoted to teacher training sessions or workshops. Faculty meetings were planned well and presented solutions to problems within the school. Parents were cooperative and caused very few problems. This attitude was transferred to students and school became a rewarding and successful experience for everyone.

Teachers weren't paid very well in those days. If your salary was around $2,400 a year, you were doing great and you got paid only once a month. So many times when my sister Mel and I finally were able to buy our sister Rose's little Chevy coupe, it sat in Maude's (our landlady) driveway and we walked to school because we had no money to put gas in it! It started to get a little better when I decided to give piano lessons several times a week and on Saturdays.

Glenn and some of our other friends continued to come to Savonna to see us on weekends. We also made some sterling friendships with several teachers that we taught with and some of the hometown people. So there were plenty of social activities to balance with our heavy school assignments. We used to go into Corning and Elmira, N.Y. to visit the nightclubs, restaurants, and the Big Band performances. In the 50's Big Band names arrived in Elmira periodically and we would not pass up a chance to go to enjoy their music. Bands such as Harry James,

Gene Krupa, Tommy Dorsey, Benny Goodman, and Woody Herman performed at a dance pavilion in Elmira. These times would be the highlight of our weekends. This was an unforgettable era—good times, good music and good schools.

Before I leave this part of the school story, I must point out that the principal of Savonna Consolidated School was a real warm dedicated person with a wonderful family. Ed and Verna Clark were two of the best school people I've ever met.

Ed Clark, principal and Verna, his wife and Kindergarten teacher, were there because they were interested in children. The teachers he hired were willing to carry out the duties assigned for the love of teaching children.

Principal Clark was there enjoying and happy with what he was doing. This was not a steppingstone or a political issue with him. He took time to get to know his teachers, parents and students. Very often he and Verna would invite teachers and others to an informal dinner and we would spend a pleasant evening with them. He was undoubtedly the best school administrator I've ever had the privilege of working with. Ed Clark was a beautiful blend of leader and humanitarian that you don't often see anymore in the scholastic world.

I stayed in Savonna for three years. Mel and I reluctantly decided to resign because we wanted to be closer to home. Dad and Mom were both getting older and health problems began to nag at them. So we handed in our resignations and one school board member called us to make an appointment with him. He offered us a higher salary if we would stay, but he was understanding enough when he found out our reason for leaving.

Chapter IX

THE SECOND SCHOOL ADVENTURE: FRANKLINVILLE AND BRADFORD, PENNSYLVANIA

With bittersweet feelings we started for home. It was good to be back. Now the search was on to find new teaching jobs. We had New York state licenses but we would have to get Pennsylvania ones if we landed jobs in Bradford, as we hoped to do. Well, as it turned out, we both had applied to the Bradford school system. Typical to my bad timing, as I found out as I journeyed through life, it was the wrong time for anyone who had not been in the service to apply for high school positions. Elementary jobs were open. In 1953-54 ex-GI's had taken most of the high school positions and jobs were scarce. But as it turned out, I had applied in Franklinville, New York, which was the next town closest to Olean, New York and closest to Pennsylvania—that would put me about fifty some miles from home. So that is where the path of my life led me.

My assignment was English, History and Social Studies classes. It was at this time that I met my future husband. Mel and I still lived together that summer after we had left Savonna. I enrolled in St. Bonaventure University for some post-graduate work. To help out at home, Mel and I took jobs at a restaurant called Neal's in Olean. During the week we lived in Alleghany because of my classes at the University and our job at Neal's.

The city bus that serviced Olean and Alleghany area made regular stops at Neal's. It was here that I served my first cup of coffee to Gene. He drove the bus and was the morning announcer on the Bradford radio station WESB. It was a great and exciting summer! We went dancing at the polka clubs in the area and often spent time at Lake Cuka located between Olean and Franklinville. On weekends, Mel and I always went home. This turned out to be a definite turning point in our lives.

Mel was hired to teach an elementary grade in Bradford, but my destiny was Franklinville and so I left to teach there. Again it was a New York centralized school. The high school curriculum was a core curriculum. I taught English using all the techniques I was taught—diagramming, paragraphing, theme structure, parts of speech, use of different kinds of sentences, expository writing, editorials, letter writing, short stories, and classic literature. High school students' courses consisted of History—U.S. and World, Geography, General Math, Business Math, Algebra, Trigonometry, Typing, Home Economics, and Shop and plenty of extra curricular activities. The students, as in Savonna, were all excellent. They seemed to enjoy coming to school. Dropouts, truancy, and discipline problems were at a minimum. Schools must have been doing something right. The usual attitude of the students was to achieve as much as possible in school and some worked after school jobs and they still managed to enjoy life and have fun participating in healthy, well-rounded activities: swimming, tennis, baseball, dancing—square dancing was particularly popular then.

The year at Franklinville High School was very enjoyable—good students, good classes and close enough to home so that I could get there every weekend. Mom and Dad were doing pretty well then and Mel and I were there to help them.

Then it was time for my sister Margie to finish airline communications school and her first assignment was in New York City—Jamaica. Mother was so nervous about her being there that I convinced myself to resign teaching and travel onto NY City Bayside where Margie and I got an apartment together.

Now I had to find a job. Teaching jobs were scarce and everyone kept telling how difficult it would be for a young girl to teach in most of the N.Y. City schools—so when an opportunity came along to work at an advertising company in Manhattan, I took it. For one and a half years, I trained in advertising. It was interesting and I did learn a great deal about business and the great opportunities that would lie in that field if you were to pursue it. But I missed teaching and I did not feel relaxed living in a large city especially when I was taking required orientation courses that would have me coming home between ten and eleven o'clock at night. Riding on the subway was scary. The subway would let us off and then I had to catch a bus that would take me to within two blocks of our apartment building. That meant walking by myself late at night. Of course being an unseasoned country bred girl, this was a very scary thing.

When Margie got transferred to Florida, I was quick to decide to leave N.Y. City and get back into teaching away from the big city. It was timing. New Britain, Connecticut, about one hundred miles from N. Y. City needed teachers.

I applied, sent in my resume and immediately was scheduled for an interview in August before the 1953-54 school year. I had such a good feeling on my way to New Britain. It was like going home.

When I arrived I was fortunate enough to get lodging with a nice Polish family. Housing was not too plentiful. This was in the 1950's and there were not too many apartment buildings or condominiums like there are now. Once settled in, I went to my first orientation meeting at the Burritt Hotel on the corner of Washington and West Main Street. It was a lovely, large room where school officials greeted us and new teachers were treated to a tasty luncheon and given their assignments for the afternoon meetings with their building principals.

Lester Levine, who was principal at the Washington Junior High School, approached me and said he had selected me to fill the Washington vacancy instead of going to Nathan Hale Junior High that I had previously been assigned. I had been in town long enough to know Washington was considered the "tough" junior high in town.

At first, I was a bit shaken and disappointed.

"Miss Napolitan—I have spoken for you to be on our staff at Washington." Mr. Levine informed me.

With his bright, blue eyes and winning smile, I couldn't show how disappointed I was and thought he must be a great person to work for. So my fate brought me to Washington Junior High.

Once inside the doors of this "rough school" I couldn't imagine how it had gotten such a bad reputation. The teachers were all friendly and excellent in their respective fields. The discipline was very good and the students, at least most of them, were diligent, caring, ready and willing to do what task was given to them. I quickly got to know most of the parents. It wasn't long before an excellent supportive group of parents was organized and functioning. Because parents were so interested and helpful in the various activities in school, the students followed suit.

These I recall as the "Golden Years" of school. Teaching was exciting and pleasurable. Due to an outstanding administration and a very cooperative faculty, we were able to do many hands-on activities that demonstrated student creativity and supported academic achievement. One example was the Student Education Fair. It encompassed all departments and subjects in the curriculum. This usually occurred in the spring of the year a month or so before school recessed for the summer. Students and teachers were alerted and preparation and arrangements were made as early as October. One of the major components of Washington Student Academic Fair was the very active parent group. They worked diligently collecting prizes and baked goods for the featured raffle, cakewalks and games that were enjoyed by the complete student body and their parents. Judges were selected from the outstanding officials from the school administration and from town officials. They would select three outstanding projects from each of the departments where students had submitted their best creative work in hopes of winning a blue, red, or white ribbon.

Our first cluster group of teachers was the backbone of the Fair: Bob Francini—English, Bud Phelps—Math, Peter Kummer—Science, and I handled Social Studies. All of us made sure to include the areas of Reading, Special Education, Home Economics, Industrial Arts, ESL, Music and Art.

It was a busy time and all of us looked forward to this big spring event.

Because it was an on-going activity that took most of the school year to prepare and plan, most students were willing and eager to stay in school to work on their various committees for decorations, designing booths for display, preparing videos, and working on layouts of materials. These committees met regularly with the faculty in charge after school hours.

From the 1950's to the 1960's brought great changes in my life.

It was then in the middle of the "golden" school years that I met one of my best friends. She also taught at Washington Junior High, Helen Yinshanis. It was during this time that I began to see Gene more frequently and started to include him into some school social events. This was probably a fairytale time of my life. I had a wonderful job, great school colleagues to work with, and a very good friend in Helen. We began to do many school and social activities together. She indeed was like another sister to me.

Gene also became a focal part of my life in the fifties. There were some turbulent times in our lives, and I quickly found out that he was very jealous and domineering at times. It took about three years to decide to say "yes" to his marriage proposal. So in 1957 my life changed dramatically. I became a Mrs. and my home was Sunrise Avenue, New Britain, Connecticut.

My first three years of marriage was a storybook life. To add to this wonderful job, colleagues, and best friend Helen, I had Gene who was a fun-loving, devoted husband. I really felt joy and accomplishment in my life.

School dropout was not a big problem in the late 1950's. In the late 50's and early 60's along with the "hippy revolution" and "do your own thing" philosophy, came the new school philosophy. Hundred of programs hit the school markets and began to inundate the school curriculum.

I began to feel a little overwhelmed and uncomfortable with so many new innovative programs being thrust upon us. But I decided to give them all a fair try to see if any were worthwhile or could compare to programs like the old phonics system that had worked for me and many of my students over the years.

In 1965, the SRA Reading Program appeared. It had been developed by Goldberg & Rasmussen and was based on linguistics and learning psychology theory. This learning theory said that the child could best learn inductively rather that deductively. Early reading should be simplified by teaching words that a child knows and uses in a sentence pattern. Patterns would be used to teach words from the most regular to least regular.

This was about to change. Our beloved and respected principal Lester Levine became assistant superintendent in New Britain and Washington Junior High School had a new principal. Situations changed. Helen and I decided to apply for positions at the high school.

On the day we were to go for our assignments at the High School, I had not been feeling well and had gone to see the doctor. Surprise! I was not going to be a teacher but I was going to be a Mommy.

When I found out that I had to resign my teaching position because of my pregnancy I was not too devastated because I was going to have this child of my own. I began planning for the baby. No joy could take the place of the expectancy of this new life that was about to join our family.

Chapter X

AT HOME

September 1960 arrived along with a new school year. The buses were out that first day of school and I felt a little left out. I was going to miss what had been the best part of my life for 33 years. I had to adjust. I had to fill my life preparing for that new little person that would eventually become the focus of my life.

I stood at the window forlorn and weepy as the old orange school buses rolled by. But I kept telling myself that a greater joy and happiness was coming inside of me. I had consoled myself and went about the daily tasks. I was interrupted by the phone ringing.

A premonition brought out some urgency and I picked up the phone. It was Margaret Murphy who was the secretary and I might add, the "nuts and bolts" of Washington Junior High School.

Margaret asked, "Terry, have you put in your resignation yet?" I said "No." I do have it ready though to go out this week.

"Hang on to it then and come down to my office. We have to talk."

I knew then that my school days were not over just yet.

It was a beautiful September morning when I headed towards Washington Junior High School. The buses had not started to roll in yet. I knew Margaret would be there early with her basket and her little dog. We greeted each other and Margaret motioned me to go into the book closet adjoining the main office while she settled her little dog. I knew then that something "big" was about to happen. It was. Margaret looked me over and said you are really not showing that much for six months and with the right clothing, I think we can do this.

"Do what, Margaret?"

She explained that the Art teacher had called in the day before school was to start. She would not be returning. Mrs. Murphy told the principal not to worry. She would get a replacement until they would be able to hire a permanent Art teacher. They both agreed that I would be it if I felt well. And so happily, I was back in school.

In the 60's, it was not permitted for female teachers to be pregnant in the classroom. I loved being back and with my smocks and loose clothing no one was the wiser. So I enjoyed the students, loved the Art classes but all this came to a jolting halt one morning when I was forced to call in to school to tell them I was on my way to the hospital and probably would have to quit.

I did and full focus came to bear on my little one. I had developed some rather serious symptoms that the doctor said would take some careful care if I were to deliver this baby in December.

It was a cold, snowy winter. There had already been two major blizzards. One was on December 12th and an acquaintance of mine who also was expecting had to be brought to the hospital in an ambulance because the storm was so intense. I kept wondering what December 24-25, when my baby was due would be like. Luckily she decided to come early. On December 21st, I went to the hospital and 18 hours later I had my precious little baby girl. I knew then that she would be the jewel of my life. I have not been disappointed.

I had turned in my resignation and by now I was reconciled and happy to do so because I had this precious little girl to care for. I spent every waking minute with her. We named her Carole Jean because she was a Christmas baby and after her father because he had been wishing for a girl long before she was born.

The boys came along in my time at home. 1962 brought Stephen and we were blessed with Michael in 1965. This was a challenging time in the 1960's. Things, people and concepts in our culture were rapidly changing.

One of the outstanding music fads was the Beetles. Their ballads had a dynamic effect on the music of our country and upon the younger generation. Music in the country was definitely changing and so were our young people. Being so occupied with the care of my three children I really didn't realize how quickly and how much our culture was changing. The phrase, "I have to find out who I am" was heard often. Young people began to form groups—some known as Hippies, groups living out in the open city parks and wherever temporary shelters were found. Children became more defiant and many left home to join these groups and roam about the country. Music changed. It became wild and frenzied reflecting the passions and emotions of the times. Young people began to take on extreme and outlandish looking fads for hairstyles and clothing. Worst of all schools and curriculum changed. Change isn't always bad but this change was not for the better.

New fads in Reading developed that did not always promote the tried and true Phonics method. Each year came a glowing promise to raise reading scores by introducing a new Reading program or a new Math program. These were expensive. They required purchasing new materials and books, training courses for the teaching staff all of which put a huge drain on most local school budgets. This required the school boards to cut some basic training programs down or entirely out. Special areas that were very important to many students that did not excel in academics were denied training in the arts of Physical education curriculum that had to be cut or eliminated in order to accommodate these new programs.

The SRA (Standard Reading Assessment) program was based on the linguistic and leaning psychology theory. It stressed that earliest reading should be simplified by teaching words a child knows in sentence patterns that they would use. These patterns presented orally and in writing. The basic aim of this program was to teach a child to decode words in sentences that are meaningful to them. This series was designed for six year olds with average intelligence and normal language skills. The SRA program had some really good features, but so did the ones they discarded.

Some of the new programs did not reach most of our growing population of minority students. These students were often shuffled off to Special Education groups or Bi-lingual groups where they stagnated and stayed for years without making significant progress in reading, writing or speaking the English language.

A number of these new programs originated in the 60's, 70's, and midway through the 80's. The linguistic reading and learning programs appeared. The Linguistic Science Readers consisted of studying language in terms of internal structure based on phonetic principle, developing comprehension, discriminating, and word patterning skills. Words were introduced in patterns except sight words. It was based on repetition and consistency.

Programmed Reading followed the theory of the "Linear" program. This program was written in frames to assure a very high probability that responses made by students would be correct.

"Peabody Rebus Reading Program" introduced children to reading by learning vocabulary of rebuses in place of spelled words. Rebus was derived from the Latin word—meaning thing. Linguistically, a rebus is a symbol or picture that represents an entire word or part of a word in contrast to letters, which represent sounds. Rebus may be pictorial, geometric or completely abstract.

The "Unifon" method developed in the 50's and used until 1960-65 by John R. Malone. It consisted of a 40-letter alphabet that utilized capitol letters only. It had uniformity-phonemic sound representation of English language, guided by a set of rules to use. This method was mostly used in business, commerce and computers.

Next came "Words in Color" devised in 1957 and copyrighted in 1962. This was a program for teaching reading in which every sound of the English language is categorized into a particular color regardless of its spelling. There were 280 different instances of graphs and digraphs creating 47 sounds in the English language. Each sound was color-coded. It was considered a good teaching method for students with reading disabilities such as dyslexia.

"The New Streamlined English Series" developed from the original Laubach Method. This method was copyrighted in 1969 and revised in 1973. It attempts to utilize the visual, auditory and kinesthetic input learning modalities and the verbal, vocal and fine meter output modalities.

All of these methods of leaning had some good qualities and some disadvantages to the learner. None had all the benefits of the original phonic system. Later, this was proven by a drop in reading proficiency and lack of interest in reading. The magic of reading was disappearing rapidly along with the ability to do simple math without pencil and paper.

In the 1960's James S. Coleman author of The Coleman Report, presented his writing largely based on school segregation, which stated that minority students learn better in integrated schools. Later he completed another study on school integration that caused a great deal of controversy and created a large influence on education as did his first one which stated that "programs of desegregation have acted to further separate minorities from white students rather than to bring them together". He further stated "The blame lies largely in the forces of massive bussing." [1]

These writings of Coleman kicked off a tremendous explosion of educational opinions that dealt with subjects such as Peers, School Quality and Achievements.

The Coleman Report has been criticized for its methodology. But many of the basic findings in it have been confirmed. Mostly, measuring attributes of teachers and schools have not been systematically related to student performance. [2]

In 2004 the federal government began expanding its role in providing compensatory funds for disadvantaged students under the Elementary and Secondary School Act of 1965. This was renewed and became the "No Child Left Behind Act" of 2001. [3]

These were some of the problems that were faced by school administration and teachers in 2000—none of these suggestions and newly created programs and policies seemed to produce the necessary goals that schools aspired to achieve.

This was the all-consuming problem that faced teachers in the 70's.

[1]   James S. Coleman Report 1967

[2]   Hanuschek 2003

[3]   Bowles & Levin 1968, Cain & Watts 1970, Hanushek & Kain 1972

Chapter XI

BACK TO THE BOOKS

With my children now in school and conditions at home getting a little rough, I decided to try to get my old job back at Washington Jr. High School. By this time our well-respected Principal, Lester Levine, was now the assistant superintendent of schools. I felt free and comfortable to go to him and ask what were the chances to get into my old school again. He gave me a lot of encouragement and several days later I got the call from Mr. Kelly, Principal of Washington Jr. High, to come in for an interview. I was delighted.

After having been accepted, I wondered if I would be able to handle increasing difficult situations at home with the new school job. A school job to me was not just 6 to 8 hours a day, but one that would take all the time needed to do the necessary work to solve all the problems and meet student needs.

"Oh well, it was worth a try."

I quickly blended into the school day. There were severe adjustments that had to be made and I can't say that I didn't come home many days feeling a deep disappointment and frustration with school and life in general. The 60's had left its mark of egotism, drugs, vandalism, vagrancy and a sharp rise in crime on society including our students. There was a marked increase on sexuality and sex in general spilling over into our student population. This, of course created many new problems.

One of the new requirements was that teachers had to get a Master's Degree and continuing upgrading on teacher certification if they expected to retain their jobs. So I rolled up my sleeves and tried to balance home life, care of an ailing mother-in-law, three growing children, school degree and upgrading certification. It wasn't easy.

It was at this time, that schools began to try to remedy the ills of society. More innovative programs were introduced into the classrooms. A small percentage of these programs were successful for the most part, but most failed to achieve positive results. More and more programs came into the schools program to reach different goals. Most failed and student issues were not improved. More and more money was needed to install these programs and many hours of teacher training were required.

Society seemed to be pulling in the opposite direction to what schools were trying to accomplish. Very little parent support was visible; TV family programs began to disappear being replaced by controversial subject matter and talk shows. Movies became more immoral and violent. Society in general became more promiscuous with older adults leading the way. In school, students began to languish in Bilingual classes for longer periods of time than was required. There was a general loss of teacher dedication along with less Reading required and a general lax in academic standards. This all resulted in student failures. It looked like public education was doomed.

Chapter XII

RECONSTRUCTION OF THE EDUCATION SYSTEM IN THE 1980'S

In the 1980's most of the reconstruction started in the building and renovating of existing schools. Educators and teachers had begun to realize that something had to be done to meet the individual needs of the diverse population that now entered the schools. Teacher certification again was upgraded. Beyond that, teacher certificates that had been issued to teachers completing their first years of successful teaching (Provisional Certificates) had to be surrendered. Professional Certificates were to be issued after the completion of 9 hours of CEU's (continuing education units) that teachers would have to earn to continue in their positions. Teachers' salaries were gradually being raised.

To try to meet the needs of students better, new computer rooms were introduced. Handicapped classes were also ushered into the public schools. More teacher aides were hired and fewer volunteers became visible. Magnet schools were stressed as well as parents and student choices. Intern programs for student teachers from various colleges were introduced. This was, perhaps, the best of all well-intended programs. These student teachers brought in fresh, new ideas to develop learning with hands-on methods. Students rapport and interest was restored somewhat in a few classrooms.

Still this was not enough to meet the needs of the overwhelming number of inner-city students that dropped out of school or those that were able to skim through, graduating with little or no reading, writing or math skills.

Schools were nearing the end of the 20th century. Students' academic progress continued to go down each year. Not only test scores but also student performance steadily decreased. Retailers, stores, offices, hospitals and almost every place of employment began complaining about the inadequacy of these young people filling various jobs.

Most schools had steadily lowered standards and instituted curriculum to appease parents and some liberal educators. Courses were introduced to help students feel good about themselves, build egos and to find out who they were. Families were falling apart. One-parent families began to be the norm. This all had a tremendous impact on student learning. Students were not getting the support and help at home that they needed and parents began to lose control of their children. Discipline became a major problem in most classrooms. Focus was on discipline and very little learning was accomplished.

I was nearing my retirement years. Discouraged and frustrated, the focus was on the CMT's (Connecticut Mastery Test). A large gap began to exist between the inner-city students and the suburban students.

With a lot of thought on this important subject of how to help inner-city school children especially, it became the focus in my life.

A plan began to formulate in my mind. Gradually I started to write these thoughts down to form and reconstruct a plan that could be interesting enough, and more importantly, work for students.

It was drastic and would require a whole change in the structure of the school day. Once completed, I revised it many times until it became crystal clear.

This plan was briefly sketched and outlined to form goals and objectives. The key rationale for these goals and objectives was first to accommodate "latch key" students who would be by themselves with peers or alone at home. One of the most important items was to provide a longer school day to include a schedule of special classes, activities, sports, homework areas and games. The idea was to get more teenagers off the streets and into a regular school supervised schedule of planned activities. An equally important goal was to maximize the already existing programs, not necessarily to add more. It would require adding personnel, and teachers to do the job needed.

This is what we need to do:

1. Have two teams of teachers—core subject teachers and special subject teachers

2. New school hours—8:00am to 6:30pm

3. More teachers and teaching aides—improve programs already existing

4. Smaller classes with inclusion in the middle school—15-18 maximum class size

5. New schedules for the day divided into two parts—Core Subjects 8:00am-1:00pm Special Subjects, homework, activities, computer 1:00pm-6:30pm

6. Establish a lab that can concentrate on Reading, Writing and Math for students not up to grade standards.

For the large number of students entering middle school that did not meet 6th grade standards in Reading, Writing and Math, these students would be required to enter a special section of the school set aside called "The Lab". Here students would be taught a concentration of Reading, Writing and Math without *any* interruption except for lavatory trips and drinking fountains, until noon—lunchtime. At this time, they would join the other students for lunch and afternoon classes for specials, school activity groups, sports, homework help and intramural sports.

All students would then be able to go home with homework done and be able to spend free time with family and friends. Parents coming home after work could pick up students at school and those needing a ride home would have buses provided.

As soon as students were able to meet grade standards in the Lab, they then would join other students in their regular classes.

This was my dream—but time was running out. I desperately tried to present a sketchy outline of this new plan to help students in middle school achieve what must be gained before they reached high school. Most would become discouraged dropouts or passed on lacking the necessary basic skills only to become unsuccessful job employees. These students needed to be given a chance to master the basic skills of Reading, Writing, and Math before high school.

An attempt was made to present this plan to Superintendents, Administrators and teachers only to be rebuffed or ignored. These were frustrating days. I then presented this plan to students and some parents. Students were greatly enthusiastic and said, "Why don't they want to help us? We think this would be a great way—especially getting our homework done in school." They also liked the idea of ending the school day with intramural sports and games.

Reaction from Superintendents was rejection because they did not want to be responsible for changing the school day time and format. Administrators did not want to deal with assigning the teacher schedules and extra work re-scheduling the whole school day. Teachers did not want to work the 1:00pm to 6:30pm shift to cover special classes, activities, sports and intramural sports. They not only didn't like the time slot, but also this would cut down on some of their stipends that teachers now receive for after school activities.

I even tried to contact some politicians that claimed they were interested in helping the students do better in schools. On the national and local level the information sent was not even acknowledged. Only one on the state level, State Representative Anthony J. Tercyak, took time to meet with me and discuss the proposal for improving the school process.

Needless to say, I was very discouraged hearing all these campaign declarations about helping students and education improvements, when most of them seemed to think that promoting more teacher workshops and teacher education classes was the answer to improving our school achievements. This indeed was not the case. It clearly was the students who needed the help to improve their skills. Teachers, if they had the command of the basic requirements to be hired, would through experience learn the different methods to teach students. If the new school program were put in place and the school day lengthened there would be time to teach basics and all that is squeezed into the school day without interruptions.

Time was running out for me. I could feel it in my bones—I was getting older and I still hadn't accomplished my lifetime goal—making schools much more effective to most of our inner city students' needs. Wearily, I closed my eyes and drifted off to sleep.

CHILDREN FIRST

Chapter XIII

WHAT A WONDERFUL SCHOOL WORLD THIS COULD BE

It was a gorgeous fall day. I was sitting outside enjoying the late summer weather. My retirement had been troublesome for many reasons, personal, health and financial and world chaotic events, but I had hung onto one dream that had kept me going. Something that the President had said, "No child left behind". As it stood now, not one school in our district had met state or national standards in all subjects. Overall in the state on Connecticut, the schools were divided into four groups. The first group of forty-two schools was identified because they did not meet the achievement or participation standards in Math and reading on the Connecticut Mastery Test.

In my troubled sleep I squirmed restlessly in a desperate attempt to get someone to listen to my New School Plan for Inner City Middle School Students. A new Commissioner of Education was to be introduced shortly.

A wave of encouragement swept over me. Maybe, if I can contact her, she can see the benefit of this new school format that would change the school day radically for these struggling students. Could I get to the right people to listen and consider doing a pilot program to test this plan? With things getting worse instead of better, it was worth a desperate try.

Newspaper headlines continued to read: "46% of Schools "Left Behind". State school test scores show poor progress under controversial Bush law. More than one in four students or about 27% reached state goal on all four subjects tested even though there was some improvements from the previous year, more than a third of those students failed to meet the goal on any subject."

Performance gaps continued to spread between suburban and inner city students.

An August 2003 headline reads: "Schools Listing Brings Pain". "149 State Schools Draw Scrutiny Over Test Results".

I felt that our public education system was sinking deeper and deeper into a quagmire.

Quoting from a headline in the Hartford Courant newspaper on Saturday, March 22, 2003:

"Failing City Schools Face Overhaul"

"Teachers are doing the best they can with what they have to deal with. The school is only going to be as good as the community and the people involved."

Francis Little, Parent

I thought to myself as I twisted and turned restlessly in my sleep—We could do it if we try. It would be worth contacting the new Commissioner to see if she would consider several pilot programs in the state inner city schools. At least give these students a chance to prove themselves. Given a chance, I'm sure they could be taught. Achievement alone would inspire them to do their best and they would develop a healthy competitive spirit to stay and participate in school.

Someone once said, "Terry, you are a dreamer!"

Well, maybe, that's what it takes a dream—then plant the seed and see if it grows.

I was determined to present this new school format with Goals and Objectives, Rationale and sample schedule. That next day I did just that. Low and behold! She actually accepted it read it through and said, "Maybe this would help. It's worth a try."

I woke up abruptly!

This was just a dream but somehow, I felt the excitement and increased motivation to push it forward. I would have to actually see to it that the right people who could do something would be contacted and convinced to put this plan into action.

Time was gone for me. I was fast approaching my twilight years. A lot of work had to be done along with a lot of talking, convincing and presenting. But what a gift to have been able to give our failing students the privilege and the proof that if properly changing and organizing the daily school schedule in the middle school, these students could experience the feelings of self worth and success in becoming productive and responsible citizens.

The future of America will be in the hands of our students today. They carry the torch to build strength and protect America's basic ideas of Democracy and Freedom in the world to come. It would be such a gift to be able to prepare them and give them a chance to do just that.

Get Published, Inc!
Thorofare, NJ 08086
18 December, 2009
BA2009291

Northwest Vista College
Learning Resource Center
3535 North Ellison Drive
San Antonio, Texas 78251